Starting Tennis

C. M. Jones and Angela Buxton

A Hyperion Book
Ward Lock Limited • London

© C. M. Jones and
Angela Buxton 1975

ISBN 0 7063 1972 9

A Hyperion Book
first published in 1975 in
Great Britain by Ward
Lock Limited, 116 Baker
Street, London,
WIM 2BB

Illustrations by
Juliet Stanwell-Smith

Text set in Bembo

Printed and bound in
Great Britain by Chapel
River Press, Andover,
Hampshire

BY C. M. JONES

Tennis: How to Become a Champion
Match-winning Tennis
Improving your Tennis: Strokes and Techniques
Your Book of Tennis

Bowls: How to Become a Champion

7.50

Contents

Introduction

The idea of this book arose from a radio programme in which problems were put to a panel of sporting celebrities. One schoolteacher bemoaned the fact that she had many promising pupils but her region possessed only minimal sporting facilities. What could she do?

Three of the panel responded pessimistically. The fourth member was Alan Davidson, one of the most famous cricketers ever produced by Australia. At first sharing her laments, he then added thoughtfully, 'When I was chosen to represent New South Wales I had never played first-class cricket and had only seen it live six times. I learned to play by studying pictures and films and reading books.'

This stimulating reply provoked the realization that stars like Mike Davies, Roger Taylor, Angela Mortimer, Gerald Battrick and Ilie Năstase came from areas where tennis is scarcely played and facilities are almost non-existent. Yet they overcame these difficulties to achieve glittering success and world fame.

The thought about Davidson and his books refused to die. Would it be possible to write and illustrate a book specially conceived to help young players lacking the opportunities for coaching, practice and competition to emulate Davidson in jumping directly from obscurity into top-class play?

In tennis Clarence Jones had coached and guided Angela Buxton from novice to champion in a breathtaking two and a half years although she had begun with technical defects acquired through learning without guidance. Neither of her parents played tennis—could they have been shown methods of preventing her technical weaknesses from developing and how to provide game-developing exercises without actually holding rackets themselves?

Many of the systems used by Clarence Jones in coaching Angela Buxton dispensed with the use of a racket and she was well beyond the beginner stage. Slowly the idea grew —and so this book came to be written. It makes no claim that every reader will one day become a tennis 'Alan Davidson'; that would require characteristics derived from hereditary factors, environment and a dedicated ambition. But it does ensure that any young would-be player who reads it, either alone or in conjunction with a parent or mentor, can acquire a technical soundness that should quickly develop into a competitive competence if he or she has the determination and ability of a Mortimer or a Taylor to overcome environmental handicaps. This will provide an invaluable foundation for it can safely be asserted that competitive success comes from confidence and confidence grows out of competence.

Our hope is that this book will teach you to acquire the first factor in this equation for success: competence.

1 Before you play

Ken Rosewall is one of the best tennis players there has ever been. He began hitting a ball against a wall when he was only three years old. Angela Mortimer won Wimbledon in 1961, but she hardly played tennis until she was nearly sixteen.

So, really, it doesn't matter very much when you start to play, providing you possess good ball sense and you begin when YOU feel the time is right for you.

We, the authors, hope you will want to have a go before you have finished reading this chapter.

Some children are born with better ball sense than others, but unless it is used it cannot develop.

The best years for development are from one to seven years old. Then the more you throw, catch, hit, kick and spin a ball, the better you will come to know how a moving ball behaves; you will learn ball sense.

But do not worry if you are older and have not played with a ball much. Perhaps you are naturally gifted and will quickly catch up those of your friends who have. Or maybe your concentration and ability to work hard will be better than theirs. Just remember that to become adept in knowing how a ball behaves you must keep on bouncing, catching, hitting, throwing and spinning one until its movements become second nature to you.

It is never too late to start the kind of ball games played by small children. A good one for improving dexterity is to stand 6 feet away from a smooth wall and to throw

1 Stand 6 feet away from the wall with the ball in your right hand. Throw the ball underarm on to the wall and catch it in your left hand. Throw with your left hand and catch with the right, continuing right, left, right, etc. Discover how many catches you can make in half a minute.

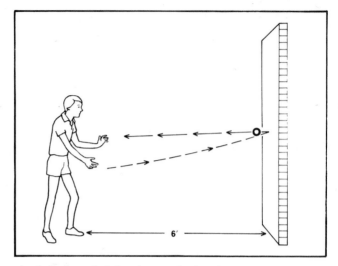

the ball from left hand to right hand, right hand to left, left to right off that wall. The ball must be thrown underarm. Ask someone to count how many changes from one hand to the other you can make in half a minute. Once you reach 20 you are becoming quite quick and skilled.

Bouncing the ball on to the ground helps, especially when you bounce it from hand to hand. If you can swing your leg over the ball without missing a bounce that helps also. Swinging each leg alternately over the ball is even more helpful. That is a good exercise for helping co-ordination.

However, such exercises may help you to develop ball sense, but they do not teach you to make tennis strokes. Tennis strokes are ultimately learned with a racket in your hand, but there are some extra exercises which we will write about later that help you progress from the simple ones you have just read about towards actual tennis strokes.

Most children are born mimics, so watching tennis on television or films, but especially 'live', helps development of strokes, particularly in the early stages. The closer you can get the better and you cannot get much nearer than in ballboying. This is how many great players like Stan Smith and Björn Borg first made contact with top class tennis. Anyone who has the chance of ballboying should take it.

Ballboying offers four possible advantages:

1 You are actually on the court so you get the same kind of view as the players of the ball's speed, length, height and direction.
2 You are in a similar position to the players and so obtain an important, close-up view of how they produce their strokes.
3 You are helping the players get on with the game and this results sometimes in your receiving small but useful pieces of equipment as gestures of their appreciation.

2 Most tennis clubs have sticks 1 yard long for measuring the net but if one is not available a standard racket length and width can be used like this.

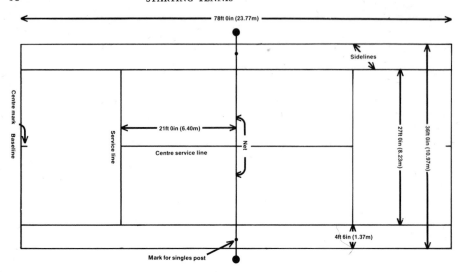

78ft 0in (23.77m)

Sidelines

Centre mark

Baseline

Service line

21ft 0in (6.40m)

Centre service line

Net

27ft 0in (8.23m)

36ft 0in (10.97m)

4ft 6in (1.37m)

Mark for singles post

3 Tennis-court
measurements

4 Occasionally one of the players will ask you if you
would like to hit a few balls with him.

If you are truly keen you will soon learn to measure the
net and have it ready for the players when they come on
court.

At tournaments there should be a suitable yard stick by
the umpire's chair, or net post. The net should be 3 feet
(0·91 metres) high in the centre and 3 feet 6 inches (1·07
metres) at the posts. These should be 3 feet outside each
sideline. This means either moving the actual posts each
time there is a change from singles to doubles, or vice
versa, which is hard work. So it is customary to issue two
spiked sticks of this height to each court. Then for singles
these can be pushed into the ground and the net supported
on them, and they can then be removed for doubles
play.

If no yard stick is available, a racket length and head
width is about the right height, but only use this method if a
stick cannot be found.

Once the net is set to the correct height, most children
wish to start playing immediately. But before doing so,

it is better that you make a brief study of the lines that mark out the boundaries of the court itself.

There are two forms of tennis: one against one—singles—and two against two—doubles. The length of the court remains the same: 78 feet (23·77 metres) with a net dividing it into two halves, each 39 feet (11·89 metres) long. For the other dimensions, look carefully at figure 3.

One more point about the court: the inner line of each set of 'tramlines' running from baseline to baseline applies to singles, the outer tramline to doubles.

The object of the game is to hit the ball within the lines so that your opponent cannot (a) reach it, or (b) return it into your half of the court.

Except when receiving service, the ball may be hit before it bounces (volleys) or after it has bounced once (ground strokes). The return of each service must be after the ball has bounced once in the appropriate 'service court'.

Any ball which falls on an appropriate line is judged 'in', even if it only touches the last tiny fraction of the line. To be 'out' the ball must miss the line completely.

A game of tennis consists of a certain number of points. A certain number of games make up a set and the majority of matches are won by the player who first wins two sets: these are called 'best of three sets' matches. A minority of men's matches are 'best of five sets', victory going to the man or two men (playing together in doubles) who first win three sets.

Each point begins with a service from the right side of your baseline to your opponent's right service court. To serve, you hit a ball from behind your baseline into the rectangle (service court) diagonally opposite you on the other side of the net.

You win the point when your service or subsequent shot hits the ball into the opponent's court and out of his reach, or if he fails to return the ball, before it bounces twice, into your court, or if he hits the ball into the net.

You lose the point if he returns your service or other stroke either beyond your reach or so you cannot put the ball back into his court, or if you hit the ball in the net.

After service each player tries to keep returning the ball until the point is won or lost.

The second point begins with a service to the left service court. Thereafter the points are played to alternate service courts: right, left, right, left, and so on.

Each game is won by the player first winning four points, except when the score reaches three points each. Then the game continues until one player (or pair) is two points ahead of the other. Then he wins the game and it is the other player's turn to serve.

Normally a set is won by the first player winning six games, except when the score becomes five games all.

Then the set continues until one player gets two games ahead of the other. The record is 49–47. However, in friendly play it may be agreed that the set ends after one further game. (You may hear this referred to as 'sudden 'death'.)

In tennis, points are not called one, two, three, etc. Traditional scoring is based on the quarters of a clock face, so:

> 1 is called 15
>
> 2 is called 30
>
> 3 is called 40 (don't ask 'why not 45?' We don't know).
>
> 4 is called game, except when the score reaches 40–40, which is called 'deuce'.

When the server wins the first point, the score is called '15 love'. (Love is used instead of nothing or nil, because the noughts on French royal tennis scoreboards were egg-shaped and players used to call out 'quinze, l'œuf', etc. And we all know how badly most English people pronounce French words.)

If the receiver then wins the second point, the score is called '15 all' (not 1–1).

It then proceeds 30–15 or 15–30, etc. Remember, one is 15, two is 30 and three is 40.

What about when the score becomes 'deuce'? Then one player must get two points ahead of the other to win the game.

If the server wins the point after deuce, the score is called 'advantage server' or, in club play, often simply 'van in'.

If he also wins the following point, he takes the game, but if he loses it, the score again returns to deuce.

When the receiver of service wins the point following deuce, the score is called either 'advantage striker' or 'van out'. If he then wins the next point, he takes the game. Losing it puts the score back to deuce, and the advantage system begins again.

There is no limit to the number of deuces in a game when traditional scoring is being used.

During the 1970s, various forms of shortened or 'tie-break' scoring were introduced into tournament tennis. However, they are hardly ever used in ordinary play and can be ignored until you are ready to become a tournament competitor.

One of the factors affecting the way you learn tennis when young is height.

Most children do not reach full height until they are about eighteen years old, and at about the age of ten they can be a foot or more short of full growth.

But a new tennis ball dropped from about 5 feet always bounces to the same height; most shots in tennis cross the net about 5 feet above ground level. For an adult this bounce will be about waist height, but to an average nine-year-old, this can be shoulder height. So unless care is taken, the nine-year-old will be learning to hit—'grooving' is the word used for constantly making a shot until it becomes a habit—shoulder-high shots.

In a few years time he will grow and so have to 'ungroove' these strokes in order to groove new ones, hitting the ball at what has become waist height. And to ungroove and then groove new strokes is more difficult than starting as a beginner.

Similarly, full physical strength does not come until full height is reached, so a normal child cannot manipulate a full-sized and weighted racket easily.

The solutions are:

1 To begin to play with balls that have lost some of their bounce. Puncturing new ones has this effect.

2 Reducing the height of the net from 3 feet to 2 feet 6 inches or even 2 feet.

3 Using one of the shorter, lighter rackets produced specially for children by some of the better manufacturers.

You have now read enough to be able to go on a court and try to play a game.

First, though, try to have another, 'reminding' look at top-class players in action on television or film. Quite a lot of teaching films are available, free of charge, to schools so, if necessary, ask your school to put on a show.

If the master is uncertain where to write, tell him to contact: The Secretary, Lawn Tennis Association, Barons Court, London W14 9EG.

When watching the film, look at the player to see what he is doing. Forget the ball. Afterwards, take up your racket, go outside and then spend a little while making imaginary strokes without a ball.

Then, if possible, find a piece of level ground with a wall by it, so you can hit a ball against it. Try to keep the ball going.

Persuade someone to watch you—but make sure they have also read this far and, if possible, they have also seen the television or film. They are supposed to have some idea of what you are trying to copy and how well you are succeeding.

When your practice session ends, be sure to collect all the balls and to leave the court or practice area tidy. Make this a habit whenever you play, no matter how good you become.

At this point, we want you to understand the feeling you should have when making the three basic strokes of tennis, namely service, ground strokes and volleys.

Each point starts with a

Service The basic feel of this action is of 'throwing' your racket face at the ball.

Once the ball is in play, the rally proceeds with:

Ground strokes These are strokes made after you have let the ball bounce once. The basic feel is of 'swinging' your racket face at the ball.

Shots hit without waiting for the ball to bounce are called:

Volleys The basic feel of volleys is of 'punching' your racket face at the ball.

To recapitulate, when serving, *throw* your racket face at the ball; when hitting ground strokes, *swing* your racket face at the ball; and when volleying, *punch* your racket face at the ball. Fix this firmly in your mind.

2 Handling your racket

It is possible to tell with surprising accuracy how far any beginner at tennis is likely to progress. However, this takes several days, involves lots of special psychological tests and skill-measuring exercises, and necessitates careful analysis by specialists. So it is a costly process. Additionally, only a tiny minority of beginners wish to know from the start if they are going to win Wimbledon or merely do well in the club championships. Most people want to play and enjoy tennis and to improve.

A rough assessment can be made by many experienced members of the Lawn Tennis Registered Professional Coaches Association. Such aptitude tests have a double use because they help the person taking them to become familiar with racket handling and also to develop dexterity.

When your racket no longer seems like a separate implement but feels like an extension of your hand and arm, you are becoming a good racket handler.

For those few who do wish to look forward a few years with greater certainty, there is a specific programme operated by the Angela Buxton Tennis Centre called 'Know your Tennis Future'. If you write to 16 Winnington Road, London N2, you will be sent full details.

Returning to racket handling, you should begin gently and take your time.

First learn to hold the racket so that you experience maximum 'feel' in your fingers and hand when the ball hits the strings.

The grip you adopt should give maximum reach and flexibility. You need all the reach you can muster to get to your opponent's best shots. Flexibility helps ball control and power. Most top-class players find that these needs are best fulfilled by holding the racket in special, clearly defined ways for the main strokes.

Starting with the forehand drive, the most effective method is called the 'eastern' or 'shake-hands' grip.

To obtain this, follow figure 4.

The forehand often becomes a player's strongest shot soonest but once you start to play matches you will find your opponents hit the ball at your weaknesses and not to your strengths.

To be more precise, they attack what *they* think is your chief weakness and so most opponents automatically aim at the backhand corner seven times out of ten.

4a Strokes made on the right side of a right-handed player are called forehands or forearms. Can you tell from this picture why?

This stroke is made with the front part of the hand facing forwards, hence forehand.

4b To obtain the customary forehand grip hold your racket in the left hand at right angles to the ground. Put your right hand against the strings.

4c Slide the right hand down to the butt (end) of the handle.

4d Now grip the handle as though shaking hands. Move the fingers until the grip feels completely comfortable.

As you will learn later, the backhand is a more natural shot than the forehand—providing you follow one or two basic rules. One of these concerns the grip.

To obtain the most secure backhand grip, follow figure 5. Notice that the ball is hit with the other face of the racket.

5a The backhand drive, so called because the back of the hand faces the ball when the ball is struck

5b *above* To obtain the orthodox backhand grip put your right thumb in the centre of your waist-line, thumb spread out, fingers together, the palm of your hand facing downwards.

5c *above right* With racket in line with the shoulders and strings at right angles to the ground, push the handle against the thumb.

5d *right* Close the hand with your thumb pointing at the strings on the back of the handle (not up the side).

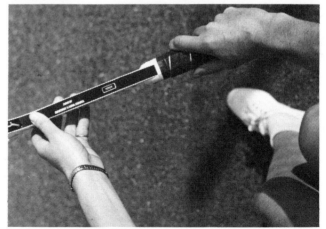

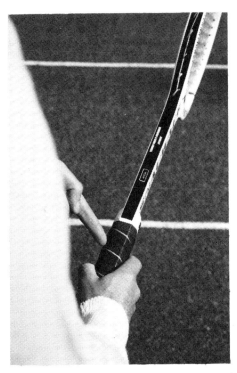

If your height is still increasing and as your game develops, you may find these two grips need minor modifications. You will also discover that there isn't always time to grip the racket in exactly the same way. This is often the case when volleying.

In between these two grips lies the best service grip. It is called the chopper grip because you hold the racket as though you are trying to chop wood with the side of the frame.

There are problems with this grip. With the exception of some young players who seem to have a special knack, it needs more wrist strength than the grips used for forehand and backhand ground strokes and volleys.

6a *above left* The chopper grip is ideal for serving. Note the position of the 'V' formed by the junction of the first finger and thumb.

6b *above* To develop racket control using the chopper grip, bounce a ball on the ground with the edge of the frame. Practise this until you can bounce the ball twenty times without moving your feet.

But strength and age don't necessarily go together: there are eight-year-olds who are very strong and thirteen-year-olds who are comparatively weak. However, you don't need any special strength to try the aptitude-developing exercise for racket handling we are about to outline, so look at figure 6 to learn the chopper grip.

7 You have read the instructions about gripping your racket. This is an exercise for use with the forehand grip but the children in the picture are making at least three mistakes. What are those mistakes?

The exercise shown in the second picture is simply to bounce a ball off the ground using the side of the racket head and keeping your wrist loose and floppy.

Before attempting this, try bouncing a ball with the strings of the racket when using the forehand grip. (See figure 7.)

Have another look at figure 7, because we want to test your powers of observation and your ability to follow instructions. Now, what is wrong with the grips of the players in the picture? When you have decided, read the answers, which are printed at the foot of this page.

After bouncing a ball on the strings of the racket with the forehand grip, try bouncing it using the backhand grip and the *other face* of the racket. If you have a friend, take it in turns to see who can bounce the ball most often without missing.

To speed up grip change, hit a ball up in the air with the forehand face of the racket while using a forehand grip. While the ball is in the air, change your grip to the backhand and then hit the ball up with the backhand face of the racket. Keep changing the face which you are using and the grip. By hitting the ball to various heights, you can give yourself more or less time to make the grip change.

At first you may have to move around to keep the ball bouncing, but once you learn to control your racket, you will be able to keep the ball going without moving your feet.

Once you can do this with all three grips—forehand, backhand, chopper—you will be ready for controlled motion while bouncing the ball.

Put four chairs or objects of any kind in a straight line, each one separated from the next by 3 or 4 feet. Start at one end and, while bouncing the ball, run in and out of the chairs from one end of the line to the other and then back again. Ask someone to time you with a watch. Try to get quicker day by day. If you have a friend who is also learning, put two rows of chairs side by side and have races; a little competition adds spice to practice.

---

1 None of the three girls on the left is using the forehand grip.

2 The fourth girl has her index finger pointing up the handle instead of around it.

3 The boy on the right is holding the racket too far up the handle towards the face.

The next stage is to find a wall to hit the ball against, keeping it going as long as possible. But that means you are ready to learn about the actual strokes used in tennis. Meanwhile, a final tip now that you should be becoming more familiar with the behaviour of a simple tennis ball: when you have to go and fetch a ball a little way away (which is done all the time in tennis) make a habit of sprinting after it; don't just dawdle, it's good for you to run and it helps you to keep in shape. Try it out and see.

3 When to hit the ball

The forerunner of tennis was called *jeu de paume* and was played with the hand. So, to capture the feel of how the primary stroke should be made, ask someone to throw a ball to you and hit it back with the palm of your hand.

If you have seen good tennis being played at your local club or tournament or on TV, you may have noticed *when* the ball is hit, nineteen times out of twenty. See if you can remember. It is, in fact, just after the ball has passed the top of the bounce and is comfortably placed at your waist height.

To make sure that you understand this very important point, ask someone to throw a loopy ball to you, underhand, a few times so that you can practice catching the ball where you intend hitting it—at waist level.

8 When to hit the ball

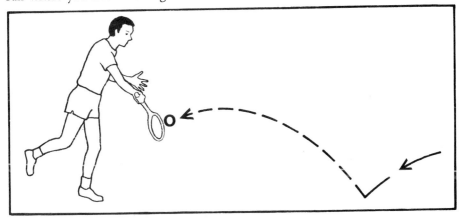

To do this you will have to judge the flight of the ball and move into the correct position. This is what tennis is all about. It is a game of continuous fluent movement.

Now try to hit the ball at exactly the same point, but using your racket instead of your hand. Make sure the ball is thrown gently to you at first.

How well did you succeed? Did your racket feel comfortable and like an extension of your arm? When you watch good players, their bodies, arms and racket all seem to belong to each other. This is the kind of harmony we hope you will succeed in obtaining for yourself.

For this reason it will probably help you if you hold your racket in the 'shake-hands' or 'eastern' grip as described for a forehand shot in the previous chapter. Now that you have hit a few balls, read the description again, to make sure that you understand.

9 You must be alert mentally and physically on a tennis court. This is the position of readiness. Legs comfortably apart and weight evenly balanced on the balls of the feet. Racket up and ready for action, the left hand supporting the 'throat' to aid quick action.

Position of readiness:

To judge and time the flight of the ball correctly, you must always be mentally alert and in the position of readiness. The most usual position of readiness is with the racket held centrally with the shake-hands grip, and spare hand at the throat.

You must be ready to move in any direction, so your weight should be slightly forward and evenly balanced on the balls of your feet. They should be placed slightly apart and facing your opponent. Your knees should be slightly bent and relaxed. (See figure 9.)

Now try hitting a few balls back to your helper again, starting from the position of readiness. Try to decide as quickly as possible where, how high and how fast the ball is travelling and move into position smoothly.

Give yourself as much time as you can for the stroke by moving your racket back early in readiness to hit the ball. Remember, you cannot swing forward until your racket has gone back.

While waiting for the ball to start on its way, you should be facing the hitter or thrower; but when you hit the ball you should be sideways to the direction you want it to go. Tennis is a sideways game.

So, as you start the forward part of the swing, step towards the ball with your left foot.

The net dividing a tennis court is 3 feet high in the middle. You have been told to hit the ball at waist height.

Waist height for most people is lower than 3 feet. So you must hit the ball upwards a little as well as forwards; the ball must be lifted.

Therefore, your swing just before and after the hit must travel upwards.

But not your head. If you jerk your head upwards you cannot see the racket strings hit the ball.

Even worse, lifting your head will lift your shoulders and you will lose control of your racket swing.

Once you have hit the ball, let your racket swing powerfully forwards to finish somewhere far ahead of your front shoulder.

Figure 10 shows a drive of this type being hit. It is called a forehand drive because the front (fore) part of the arm is facing the ball.

10 The forehand drive

But opponents do not always return the ball to the right side of your body, so you can hit it with your forehand. More than half the time they will hit it to your left or backhand side.

Think for a moment how you toss your hat into a chair or how you deal a pack of cards or play deck quoits or hoopla. Your arm crosses your body. This feels completely natural to you. It is also the swing you use when hitting the ball on the backhand.

Figure 11 shows a man hitting a backhand in the style used by most good players.

11 The backhand drive

Note from the drawings how far round the man turns away from the ball before hitting it. This is important.

To imitate this stroke, ask someone to throw some balls to you underarm and gently for a backhand stroke.

Stand with your back directly to the thrower—no half measures; all the way round—turn your head over your right shoulder and watch the approach of the ball.

Make sure you are holding your racket with the backhand grip described in the previous chapter, using your other hand to support it at the neck.

Ask for the ball to be thrown carefully so it arrives slightly to your right after the first bounce—your back is turned remember—and at the right height.

You should hit the ball just after the top of the bounce at waist level on this side too. To do this you will probably have to move. Never be frightened of moving and do start in plenty of time, always using small skipping steps. In dancing it is called chasséing. This sort of movement helps to develop good balance on a tennis court and good balance is vital for good strokes.

Start moving the instant you see the ball, with the aim of hitting the ball well out in front of you and to the side; look again at figure 11 to see how the man turns as he hits the ball.

Keep your spare hand on the racket neck until you swing into the ball and then let go with the spare hand.

Let the racket head chase the ball after the hit as if it is trying to catch up with the ball.

Figure 12 shows you how to do this exercise.

Practice aids

Student Be your own teacher by making imaginary, beautiful, flowing forehand and backhand drives in front of a mirror; this is called shadowing.

Follow the ball with your eyes, but not by lifting your head, as this forms bad habits.

Helper To make grip changes quicker, call out 'forehand swing, backhand swing, stop'. Then check student's use of correct grip. Start again, mix up the strokes, stopping periodically to check the grip.

Student If no help is available, practice on your own, by dropping the ball in front and to the side of you, letting it bounce, and hitting it into the wire netting. If there is a wall available, try to keep the ball going against it.

12a Learning the correct body turn for the backhand drive. Stand with your back to the net, racket held up and head turned to look at your helper.

12b Helper throws the ball so that it bounces and comes towards you for you to swing at and hit.

To help your timing Think to yourself in waltz time 'bounce, step, hit'. This applies to both forehand and backhand.

If you get tied up with the backhand Revert to something you know like hoopla or deck quoits until you become confident with the movement. Then use your racket again.

Improvement You will be making good progress when you can keep up a ten stroke rally, using either stroke, with a friend.

Note to helper
To check if student is really watching the ball, find half a
dozen old balls and a green, a red and a black felt marker. On
two of the balls put a couple of red spots, each about the
size of a new penny and on opposite sides of the ball. On two
other balls put two black spots and on the remaining two, ink
in green spots.

    Put them in a bag, go to one service line and put the student
—with racket—on the service line on the other side of the net.
Throw each ball for the student to hit and make him call out
the colour of the spots as he does so. He should be right at
least five times out of six.

4 The service

There is one stroke in tennis in which your opponent can do nothing to affect your performance. He can neither hurry the time you take in producing it, nor can he slow you down once you begin. The rules allow you a second try if you fail first time and it begins each point.

This is the service and you do not need an opponent to practise it so there should be no excuse for having a weak or unreliable service.

If you can throw a ball strongly with the action used by cricketers you can also develop a strong service because the action is a throwing one. You throw the head of the racket at the ball which you have tossed into position with your free hand. A better phrase is 'placed into position'.

First, then, take a box of balls and go to the baseline at one end of the court. Throw them, one after another, as far as you can over the net. How far each ball goes depends on how big, strong and flexible you and your muscles are. As a rough guide, a strong fourteen-year-old boy may throw a ball over the wire netting at the far end of the court.

In throwing make sure your arm bends fully at the elbow and that the forearm is pointing straight up at the sky during that part of the action when you actually release the ball. Throw the ball upwards.

Another way of learning the correct 'feel' of serving is to get a nail and hold it as high as possible straight in front of you as if hammering it into a wall. Holding the

13 The best services are based on a throwing action. To serve well, first learn to throw strongly like the boy in these pictures.

nail as high as possible shows you how high your free hand should go before gently placing the ball into the correct position for hitting when you deliver a real service. Placing here means guiding the ball carefully to the correct height and hitting position, which is about 18 inches (45 centimetres) above an outstretched upward-pointing arm. This is so much more accurate than throwing the ball high in the air and then trying to hit it on the way down; you will never develop a fluent service that way.

But before trying an actual service, see if you can find an old racket because we want you to imitate the correct action by throwing a racket instead of a ball as hard as you can.

So, again, go to the baseline but this time stand with your back to the net and throw the racket high into the wire netting behind the baseline. As with the ball, throw the racket in an upwards path, not straight ahead or downwards.

Make the throw as vigorous as possible; your back is towards the playing area of the court so that the old racket will not be landing on it and digging up holes.

Check that your feet and body are in the best position. Your shoulders should be in the diagonal line with the path you want the racket to travel.

That means your feet should be on that same line with the front foot pointing in the direction the ball should take. As a simple check, take up your stance and then lay your racket down on its side so both big toes are touching it. If the racket points along the diagonal line you want the ball to follow you know instantly your feet are correctly placed. If necessary move your feet around until the racket is pointing in the right direction.

Having thrown the racket a few times and sensed what it feels like to do this, try a few shadow services; shadowing means going through the entire action of serving, without actually using a ball.

We have found it best to do this in six clearly defined stages.

First, take up the correct starting position. Second, swing the right arm down so that the racket goes past the knee; keep your arm straight while you do this. Simultaneously let your left arm swing upwards in order to 'place' the imaginary ball in the hitting position. The feeling you should have is that your arms are working like scissors opening up. Third, let the swing continue until the racket handle comes down on your shoulder like a soldier's gun. Fourth, with a gentle bend of the knees and your free arm outstretched, imagine you are gently placing the ball up about 18 inches (45 centimetres) above the point where you let it go so you can hit it at full stretch. Make

sure you keep your head up so you can look at the ball all the time. Fifth, with the racket starting from the on-the-shoulder, gun position, throw the racket head at the imaginary ball—but this time don't let go. Sixth, let the racket sweep down and past your left leg.

Repeat this several times. Think about what is required in each individual movement. Do not worry if you pause between each movement. Linking up and continuity will come once you become proficient.

Next, stand three yards or so away from the wire netting surround with two balls and a racket at your feet. Take up the correct starting position and then bend down, pick up one ball and throw it into the netting to remind yourself of the throwing order. Without pausing, bend down again, pick up the racket with your hitting hand, the ball with your free hand and have a go at a proper serve into the netting.

14a *opposite top left* The starting position

14b *opposite top right* The first movement.

14c *opposite bottom left* The swing continues

14d *opposite bottom right* The ball is placed with a gentle throw into position

14e *above left* The moment of impact

14f *above right* End of service

Once your racket and the ball make contact a few times, go on the court wherever you feel you will be able to serve the ball into the service area diagonally opposite you on the other side of the net.

This could be only two or three yards from the net, or near your own service line, perhaps midway between the service and baselines or even in the correct place by the baseline.

At this stage it matters very little where you stand. You should be trying to serve the ball consistently into the correct area, and depending on your age and size you could be close to the net or near the baseline. Once your accuracy improves you will gain in confidence and then you can start moving back towards the baseline.

Strength and size are also likely to affect the way you hold your racket when serving.

Undoubtedly the best grip for serving is the one known as the chopper.

As an exercise, try bouncing a ball on the ground off the side of the racket frame, keeping your wrist relaxed and flexible while doing it. Do not move your whole arm and body; simply the wrist. (See figure 6.)

If you are strong enough to use the chopper grip when serving you will find it is necessary to turn your wrist at the point of impact so that you hit the ball where you want it—not out to the left.

To get the feel of this, stand by the wire netting and go through the service swing so that your racket hits the netting flat on, not with the strings pointing to the left.

Younger players will probably find it easier to serve with the grip they use for the forehand drive. When they can serve comfortably from the baseline they should change to the chopper grip—unless they never intend to be more than dabblers.

When you find all these points are working smoothly you will be able to develop extra power by letting your

15 Strong serving that is also consistent virtually demands the use of the chopper grip. Young children may not be strong enough to control a racket with this grip and so a change will be necessary around the age of twelve. The chopper grip necessitates turning the wrist just before and during impact. To discover the extent of the turn stand facing the court surround and 'shadow' a service, ending with your racket hitting the surround as in this picture.

racket face loosely 'scratch your back' when at position 3. The further down your back your racket drops, the greater the power, you will be able to develop—all else being equal.

Practice Aids

1 For any students meeting with great difficulty in trying to follow these instructions, we advise starting from the third position. Although we cannot recommend this service action becoming permanent we do recall that Angela Mortimer actually won Wimbledon in 1961 serving in the manner.

2 With a parent or friend, make practice fun and competitive by seeing who can hit the highest number of correct serves using twelve balls in succession. You take the right court from one end and they take the left court from the other. To add additional stimulus, place a large target near one of the lines in your service court and another target in theirs. Score 1 point for correct serve (remembering a ball on the line is in!) and 5 points for hitting the target. Then change ends and serve into the left court.

3 Helpers are not always available but you can put in useful time practising 'Do you beat yourself?'

Allow two serves per point as in a normal game. Start in the right court; if either your first or second serve goes in, the score is 15 love. Move to the left court. Should this then be a double fault, the score becomes 15 all. If either ball goes in, it is 30 love. Continue to play one set this way.

When you become more expert, a double fault can cost you the whole game instead of 1 point. Later still you need only allow yourself one serve. This incidentally is very good for second serve practice and they say a tennis player is only as good as his second service. For a final disciplined type of practice, again with one ball, a single fault costs you the whole game instead of just the point.

5 Volleying

A volley is a shot which is hit before the ball bounces. Unlike the swinging ground shot and the thrown serve, it is *punched*. Volleys are normally made near the net with the aim of winning the point there and then. So they are aggressive shots, played with an alert mind, and the racket held high for immediate action—at least it should be, but many good players are slack about this. Make sure you don't join them.

There are two basic volleys—forehand and backhand. For these we use the forehand and backhand ground-stroke grips as described in Chapter 2. To learn the correct punching action, begin with the method advocated by the many times Wimbledon champion Billie-Jean King. We find this an unfailing system.

Use the grip illustrated in figure 16a, making sure your thumb faces your opponent and the handle of the racket is acting as a 'splint' to your arm and wrist, placed right down your arm, and not sticking out on one side or the other. Now ask your helper to throw a few balls at you from across the net. As each one approaches, step forward and punch out, sending the ball for him to catch. Make the ball travel *outwards* not downwards. Keep doing this until you can punch the ball over the service line before it hits the ground though this may quickly tire your hand. If it does, stop and let your friend have a go for five minutes and then try again. That is the feel of a punched volley with the racket in front of your face.

16a *above* The Billie-Jean King system of learning to volley. Make sure the racket handle is contacting your arm along its length and that your thumb is facing your helper. After the helper has thrown a few balls underarm for you to punch back, slide your hand down the racket handle as in 16b.

Next, slide your hand down the handle with it still in the Billie-Jean style grip. (See figure 16b.) Again make sure your thumb faces your opponent.

Once more ask your friend to throw a few balls for you to volley back to him. Once you have mastered this you are ready to try volleying with the orthodox forehand or backhand grip.

You may find difficulty in controlling the ball because your wrist is now free of the 'splint' effect of the racket handle. You may even find this happening occasionally when you have become a good player. Whenever this happens go back to the start and hit a few volleys with the Billie-Jean King 'volley aid'. That should soon help you to regain control of the ball.

Now try the real thing. Stand with your back against the wire netting surrounding the court. This will prevent you swinging your racket back and force you to jab or punch at any ball. Wait in the position of readiness with the racket shoulder height and well in front; in punching the ball, it is necessary for the point of impact to be well out in front. Now shadow the stroke. Imagine the ball coming towards your forehand. As you 'see' it reaching the punching position, step forward with your left leg, your knee bent and body crouching forward. Without any backswing, *punch at the ball*. Make the racket face travel in a straight line along the path you wish the ball to go. Think of it as chasing the ball and trying to catch it. It is important for your wrist to be firm when hitting ground strokes, and even more important for it to be braced when hitting volleys, because the ball frequently comes at you fast. You are also nearer the net so you have far less time to make the shot and that means greater likelihood of mis-hits. Punch firmly and straight through the ball.

After a few shadow volleys with an imaginary ball, ask someone to stand about four yards away and throw a few balls to you at roughly the height of your shoulder. With your back against the court surround, step forward with your left foot, simultaneously punching the ball back for him to catch. Repeat this until you are confident and can really feel the punching action.

Then move on to the court itself, stand on the centre service line a little more than your racket's distance from the net, facing the other half of the court. Hold your racket up and in front of you.

Again ask your helper to throw some balls at you from just inside his service line so that you can punch them over the net, into his court, and beyond his reach.

Now that there is nothing pressing on your back to prevent it, take care not to swing the racket backwards before punching forward at the ball. (See figure 17.)

16b *opposite* Slide your hand half way down the handle using the same grip as in 16a. Again, be sure the racket handle acts as a 'splint' for your arm. Punch forwards and upwards.

Always remember when volleying that the racket *must* be punched forward to *meet* the ball out in front. There must be no question of the ball's being allowed to hit the racket at your side. Punch straight through the ball.

17 To ensure you punch the ball, stand with your back to the netting. When your helper throws the ball underarm to you at shoulder height, step forward and punch forwards and upwards.

As with the forehand, so the backhand volley is a punch in which there should be no backswing.

Keeping your playing hand in front of your face with the thumb facing your nose ensures that your racket is in a good position for rapid, protective action if the ball is hit hard and straight at you from close range. This is important because many, if not most, beginners are secretly frightened of being hit and hurt by the ball when they first learn to volley. Often that secret fear persists through their entire careers, even after they have won international championships.

18a The position of readiness for the backhand volley. The racket is held up and away from the body in a position where it can be used to punch the ball without any further movement to ball height.

18b The start of the backhand volley. Note the forward movement and the punching action. The wire netting prevents any backswing, so forcing a punch.

18c Completion of backhand volley using the Billie-Jean King teaching system. The step forward has been made and the ball is on its way back for the helper to catch.

It affects nearly every beginner, whether aged seven or seventy. That hold, especially when the free hand is used as an extra support on the throat of your racket, enables you to move the racket head very quickly in front of any tender part of you, so reducing the chances of injury to less than when crossing a busy street.

Holding the racket that way does reduce your reach on the forehand slightly but that is a small price to pay for lessening your fears.

Once more stand with your back to the court surround and ask someone to throw a few balls to your backhand side at shoulder height so you can volley them back for him to catch. As the ball comes to you step forward to meet it with your right foot. This will turn your right shoulder towards the ball. Punch outwards and straight through the ball and make your racket face chase the ball along the line you want it to go. Do not pull your racket across the ball from left to right, a common fault.

Hold your racket near its throat with your free hand as long as possible. This gives greater control and will add to the thrust if you push forward with it when you punch the ball.

Once you can feel yourself punching through the ball correctly move on to the court itself—stand on the centre service line a little more than your racket's distance away from the net.

Once more, ask your helper to throw balls at you. Punch them back over the net and inside the singles court but beyond his reach; tennis is a game in which you hit the ball away from your opponent. Cultivate the habit right from the start.

Even if you are not tall, try to punch the ball as near as possible to your friend's baseline.

Remember, no backswing but just a strong punch with your racket head following through along the line you want the ball to travel. Watch the ball carefully so your right shoulder is turned towards it and make your racket punch the ball, not just let the ball plop on to the racket.

Once you become proficient—and this should not take long—ask your helper to throw the balls haphazardly, some to your forehand, others to your backhand, so you never know which it will be.

Be alert and evenly balanced on the balls of your feet, which should be about your shoulders' width apart. Even more important than physical alertness is mental quickness. Try to see which side of you the ball will be coming the moment he throws it—or hits it if he is a player himself and using a racket.

It is surprising how many clues about direction you can discover through watching an opponent closely. The only way to learn used to be by experience but nowadays we have found ways of teaching players through our films 'Reading Lawn Tennis'.

Sometimes the ball comes to you low over the net and with spin, which forces you to play it at ankle height.

Most beginners bend at the hips to reach such returns. Wise ones learn the correct way, which is to bend at the knees, crouch down low and keep your nose as near as is comfortable to the racket face so your eyes remain as near as possible to the ball.

As with volleys hit at shoulder height, low ones must be made with a firm grip and wrist.

19a and b *opposite*
Kerry Melville and John Newcombe making low forehand and backhand volleys. Note how their knees are bent with head and shoulders well down so that their rackets are parallel with the ground. This helps ball control enormously.

Pictures: Australian News and Information Services

Because the ball has to be lifted over the net, which is three feet high at the centre band, there is danger of 'ballooning' the ball over the baseline. This tendency for the ball to fly can be corrected by using a little back spin, or slice as it is usually known.

Even though the ball may be only six inches above ground level, it must still be punched—but upwards. The controlling back spin is applied by making the racket curl slightly under the ball during the brief moment of contact. The action is a little like spooning the last few cornflakes out of your plate at breakfast. Figure 19 shows how this is done.

Practice Aids

Student Be your own teacher by making imaginary, firm
volleys in front of a mirror. Follow the ball with your eyes,
not lifting your head at all, and imagine the ball so strongly
that you follow it on to your racket strings with your eyes.
Helper To help quicken grip change, call out 'forehand punch,
backhand punch', etc. in varied sequences. Check that student is
watching the 'ball' on to his racket and that he is stepping
forward with his left foot when you call 'forehand' and right
foot when you call 'backhand'. Ensure that he is punching,
not swinging his racket.
Student Find a garden or garage wall and try to keep the ball
going by volleying against it from three or four yards away.
Hold your racket up all the time and try to move it quickly.
If you are near to the wall you will not have time for a
backswing; you will be forced to punch.
Helper Watch that the student is moving his feet and turning
his body. His movements should be easy, quick and graceful.
Ensure that his eyes follow all the time and every five or six
shots call out 'racket up'.
Student Imagine balls coming at your toes while standing in
front of a mirror. Use your knees to get down to them and
crouch from the hips and waist to keep your nose and eyes
near the racket face. Curl the racket under the 'ball' and feel as if
you are nursing it over the net.
Helper Remind the student of the correct way to bend by calling
out 'knees' quite frequently. See how near to the racket face

Sig. 4

he gets his nose and eyes. Ensure that he steps forward to meet the ball.

Student Stand at the net a little more than a racket's length away, in the readiness position for volleying. Cover only half the width of the court but use the whole length, including the tramlines. When the helper drops and hits the ball to you, try to volley it so he cannot return it. If you succeed, score one point. If he passes you or you make an error he scores one point. No high shots allowed. Play the first to reach 10 points.

Helper To drop and hit the first ball from anywhere between the service and baseline. Helper must try to pass the volleyer with every shot following the first one. No lobbing over his head.

Student: Take up a position between two of the supporting posts of wire netting surround. Stand with your back against it and your racket high. Try to prevent the helper hitting balls past you into the netting between the posts and above the height of a tennis net. This could be indicated with string.

Helper Stand about five yards away. Bounce each ball separately and try to score a 'goal' between the posts.

N.B. This is a good exercise for developing volleying agility.

Combination ground stroke/volley

Helper Have two balls in your hand. Drop one and hit it to fall in the service area on the student's forehand. Then after he has played a forehand stroke and as he comes to the net drop the other ball and hit it to his forehand for him to volley.

Repeat this exercise on the backhand.

Finally when the student becomes more proficient, mix the feeds to the forehand and backhand.

Student Stand just behind the service line, with racket ready for forehand drive. When helper hits first ball, play a forehand drive and run to the net with racket up ready for the forehand volley. When helper hits second ball try to volley it out of his reach inside the singles court.

Practice forehands till proficient then change to backhands. Score 2 points if both are correct; only 1 point if one is correct. No points are scored if neither goes in. Repeat 10 lots of two balls. Maximum score is, therefore, 20. Then swop places with the helper and feed him with 10 combinations of two. The highest score out of 20 wins.

6 Practising

This is possibly the most important chapter in the whole book—and for one special reason. It is: *Wimbledon championships are won on the practice court.*

Tournaments and championships are where you use all your strokes and strategies to win but the practice court is where you learn them. So remember our special 'Three Cs' formula. It says:

> **C**ompetitive success comes from
> **C**onfidence and confidence comes from
> **C**ompetence

Competence is knowing what to do, how to do it and when to do it, and later, when you become a good player, why to do it.

Practice means repeating some movement, sequence, or shot over and over and over and over, again and again, until your body does it of its own accord. But this is where you have to be extra careful because each time you make the movement you 'groove' the body so that it is just that tiny bit easier next time. Unfortunately, you can groove something which is wrong just as easily as something which is correct.

To put that right you have first to ungroove the wrong stroke or whatever it is before you can properly groove the correct one—which is more difficult than grooving the correct stroke from the beginning.

So when you practice to develop competence concentrate every scrap of your mind on every single shot that you make. It sounds difficult and it is. But after a short while you will discover that practising in that way is much more enjoyable than idly hitting balls backwards and forwards. There is a time limit on complete concentration. Think of it as being eight minutes. After that your brain 'goes to sleep' and you are likelier to groove wrongly than you are correctly.

But a change is as refreshing as a rest. So if you have been practising your forehand drive, change to serving for eight minutes and then go on to volleying, and so on.

Remember, too, that tennis is a game of movement and is not static. So learn from the start to hit the ball while you are moving—moving smoothly. The advanced book *Improving your Tennis* by C. M. Jones (*Faber & Faber*) reveals that there is no more danger of making mistakes when you are moving smoothly than there is when you are standing still. And so to details.

There is no more reliable practice opponent than a wall. Search your district to find one with a piece of flat ground facing it. Then, if it is necessary, seek permission to use it.

One problem often found with otherwise beautifully suitable walls is too little space in front. Recently this has been solved by a practice board which is covered with absorbent material so that no matter how hard you hit the ball, it never bounces back more than about six feet. With such a board you can practice your strokes for hours on end in even the smallest of back gardens.

When using a practice wall or board never forget that tennis is a game of movement so hit each ball at angles that will constantly keep you running for the return. Beware of simply hitting the ball straight forward so that you do not have to move your feet and body to hit the return. Always keep moving, easily and lightly.

As it is somewhat difficult to judge length, refrain from hitting too hard. Instead, use your wall practice time to develop rhythm and fluent style. Take care to watch each ball right on to the strings of your racket *every time you hit that ball.* It is so very easy to become automatic and unthinking when practising against a wall, especially because you can never hit the ball *out.*

Thoughtful, skilful use of a wall or board will help to groove your shots but learning how to place the ball has to be discovered on the court itself. Begin gently by asking a friend to take some balls—a dozen if possible— and stand on the service line at the opposite side of the net to you. Take up a position of readiness on the baseline if you are nearing full development, on the service line if you are small, or somewhere between if you are still growing.

Ask your friend to throw each ball, underarm and slowly, for you to hit it back over the net and towards a target near one of the lines; start placing the ball as soon as you can hit it over the net. Your friend should continue 'feeding' you in this way until you can hit nine or ten out of twelve over the net and in the direction of the target. Then ask him to hit balls at you with a racket, hitting them deeper and faster as your proficiency increases.

Always try to aim the ball towards one of the sidelines to avoid developing the habit of hitting the ball back to your opponent. As a first ambition try to keep up a rally to ten shots, that is five shots each. Then increase to ten shots each and occasionally up to twenty-five. You must always have control, but take care not to become a 'plonker'—the name given to players who simply run fast and push the ball back until their opponents miss in despair.

To improve your accuracy and control, play a short game of ten points (first to reach ten) using the service courts only. Serve underarm from behind the service line for the first five points and then let your friend serve for the next five points, then you for the next five, and so on. Serve diagonally to the opposite service court, first to the right, then to the left, one service only per point, which should be played out.

As you improve, use only one of the two service courts. First play diagonally, then only in the two service courts facing one another.

To develop your enterprise and aggression, score three points instead of one every time you hit a shot which your opponent cannot touch.

This method of scoring three points for each untouchable shot can be used in any type of practice game you play.

But when practising in this way always score 'one, two, three', usually until you or your opponent scores ten.

Like everything else, winning is largely a matter of habit and you should begin the association of traditional (15, 30, 40, etc.) scoring with winning at the earliest possible moment—and having started it, go on developing it.

When you are not playing games like this, put targets on the court—such as tennis holdalls or large handbags etc.—and with a friend throwing or hitting balls to you, try to hit the targets.

A word of warning. Have a good look at the target before you start, then, with your head down, keep your eye on the ball, and try to hit the targets from memory.

The commonest fault in tennis, and any other ball game, is looking up to see where the ball is going before actually hitting it. So, remembering Chapter 3, visualize the position of your target and concentrate on hitting each ball just after the top of the bounce. That way you will be forced to judge, move and time the ball. This will automatically force you to keep your eyes on it.

Remember, too, the limits to your powers of concentration and do not continue with one type of practice game beyond those limits. If you cannot remember, go back to the early part of this chapter.

When you progress beyond the Lawn Tennis Proficiency Award stage—you can read about this in the next chapter—and start playing competitively, you will be wise to use what we designate disciplined practices.

For example, you may be suffering a spell in which all your best shots seem to be ending up in the net. So you arrange to play your friend ten points in which you lose two points every time you hit the ball in the net. Perhaps your friend hits too many returns out of court. Let him lose two points every time he drives the ball beyond the base or sidelines.

Are you double faulting too often? Then play ten points in which you are only allowed one service per point.

Your length is too short? You lose two points every time your drive pitches short of the service line.

There will be times when you cannot find another player to practise against. Never mind, you should still be able to find someone who will be willing to go out on the court to throw balls for you to hit. In this situation ask him to throw the balls so you have to run to strike each ball and put down one or two targets which you can try to hit.

Figure 20 shows how ten balls might be thrown to you.

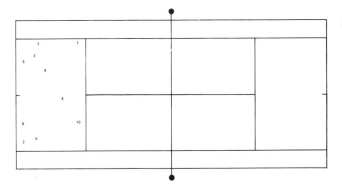

20 Shot-practice chart

You don't actually have to be on a court to practise. If you sit back in a chair, close your eyes, concentrate hard and imagine yourself playing strokes, your nervous network will behave in exactly the same way as if you were on the court.

This is called 'mental rehearsal' and it is every bit as important to imagine every little detail as strongly and correctly as when really playing. But when you do this—perhaps for ten minutes each morning and another ten minutes each night—you will, quite definitely, be deepening the 'grooves' in your muscles and nerve trains and so helping your strokes.

Billie-Jean King and Julie Heldman are two great players who make extensive use of mental rehearsal. Helen Wills, who won the Wimbledon women's singles a record-breaking eight times, used this type of training to strengthen her determination.

Every night when she went to bed she kept on saying to herself 'I can and I will. I can and I will. I can and I will'—and, my goodness, she did!

Finally, when you become good enough to play in junior tournaments, you can try a game which simulates the strange and annoying things which happen in tournaments and match play.

It is called the game of Hazards and was invented by Sheena Dalton, a senior coach at the Dudley Georgeson School of Tennis. It was reported fully in the July 1973 issue of the official LTA magazine. The article reads:

We practise our strokes and playing games but do we ever practise—or teach young players—coping with bad line calls, footfaults, arm, wrist and leg injuries and other 'slings of outrageous fortune'?

With this in mind I demonstrated a system during the 1972 LTRPCA conference at Lilleshall for introducing 'hazards' into practice match play. LT editor, C. M. Jones, pounced on the idea and, in order to encourage its development, offered me a £5 first prize and two books as 'consolation' if I would organize a 'hazards' tournament. It was staged at the Finchley Manor LTC late in March.

During the matches competitors were arbitrarily subjected to pressures related to those encountered in tournament play.

They fell into three categories:
(a) those which are likely to happen in any match;
(b) others which were greatly exaggerated but aimed at making
    the opponent think tactically about how to play;
 c) those aimed at encouraging them to 'win' rather than to
    'avoid losing'.
Some examples of these three categories are:
(a) *Injured shoulder:* player not allowed to serve overarm, volley
    or smash; must finish the match serving underarm and
    playing ground strokes only.
    Broken racket: player must go off court to find another one.
    Bad call from umpire: player loses a point she thought she had
    won.
    Footfault
    Injured leg: player must play the next game walking only.
(b) *Injured arm:* player must play next game left-handed.
    Injured shoulder: (as in (a) above) opponent must obviously
    try to bring the player up to the net, which is a tactic
    which girls especially should be encouraged to practise as so
    many baseline-hugging girls are reluctant to go near the net.
(c) The player who wins the next point wins the game (no
    time to waste valuable points here).
    Game point to you but you can only win by a service ace,
    winning volley, or smash.
Reversing the score was another 'hazard' to encourage stoicism
in the face of disappointment, and there were at least four
outside forms of pressure which applied throughout the
tournament:
 (1) They were playing for a £5 first prize.
 (2) Each match was only one set.
 (3) The rain, which was with us most of the time!
 (4) We used the Van Alen Simplified Scoring System which is a
     straightforward 1, 2, 3, 4 scoring system, with a best of
     9 points tie-break at 6 games all. The tie-break was used
     thrice during the tournament, but the greatest difference
     in this scoring system from the normal one is that there is
     no deuce. At 3 points all, the next point decides the game;
     similarly, at 4 points all in the tie-break, the next point
     decides the match.
Later all the players were asked ten questions after the tourna-

ment. They all answered them intelligently and very carefully, and gave good reasons for their replies. An analysis of these replies shows:

(1) All enjoyed the tournament, in spite of the hazards, and except for the score-reversing one and the left-handed one, felt it was realistic and not just a new party game. They also felt quite happy about VASSS, although the 'no-deuce' rule was quite different and took some getting used to.

(2) They all felt that practice of this kind would be good for their tennis and would help them to take natural hazards encountered in matches in their stride.

(3) The reaction to the 'walking only' hazard for the opponent varied between making it easy for the player to place the ball away from her to win the point, and making the player over-conscious of this and so tending to hit the ball too wide and losing points instead.

(4) Most thought that their opponents exploited the weaknesses brought about by the hazards well (e.g., drop-shotting when the opponent was not allowed to volley, to bring them up to the net). This is good, because it shows that they were all thinking positively.

(5) They did not seem to feel that their normal game was upset between hazards, and in one case, a player felt that having to come off the court in the middle of a match actually helped her to regain concentration which had been slipping.

Since then this hazard game has been developed and the following have been added by the Angela Buxton School:

1 *Lacking confidence in serve?* Student to play one set using one serve only.

2 *Put off by outside conversations and activities?* Student must learn to finish rally even when suddenly told to stop play or there is a sudden burst of clapping or stampeding nearby.

3 *Put off by introduction of new balls?* New balls to be regularly and deliberately introduced in the middle of practice sets.

4 *Put off by bad administration by umpire?*
   (a) Student suddenly told to change ends during the middle of the game, umpire seemingly having forgotten it earlier.
   (b) Student suddenly told to take off two points. Now, instead of leading, he is behind, and told to continue playing regardless.

5 *Put off by footfaults?* Student footfaulted at random—even if he is not—and play to continue without argument.

6 *Too lazy to remove all stray balls on or near the court?* Points automatically taken from student for each ball spotted on or near the court during play.

7 *Lazy mover?* Student to put on climbing boots for two games to impair movement even more. Afterwards perhaps he will find ordinary moving easier.

8 *Fear of using serve/volley technique?* Student to play two service games with each serve to be followed by a volley.

7 Gaining proficiency and joining a club

Only a few people who take up tennis remain content merely with social-recreational play. The vast majority develop some competitive ambitions, even if they do not progress beyond the stage of beating the local doctor and his wife 'who are a bit self-satisfied with their tennis'; this is a real example taken from one of our pupils.

Youngsters, of course, think more ambitiously but tournaments are costly, both in time and money. Many children can only compete in two or three tournaments a year and some cannot even manage one. Additionally, until recently, 'fourteen and under' encompassed all children from four to fourteen, so that the ten-year-olds were at a serious physical disadvantage when competing in this age group.

For these and other reasons the Lawn Tennis Registered Professional Coaches' Association gave the subject long consideration and in the 1960s evolved the Lawn Tennis Performance Award Scheme.

Based on the medal system used in ice skating and ball-room dancing, its official object was 'to further interest in Lawn Tennis, particularly with the younger generation. The Scheme consists of an examination open to anyone, aimed at setting a standard of performance'.

In broader terms, the scheme has its greatest appeal when a youngster has progressed from the beginner stage to one where he can join a club and take part in games with other members without spoiling their pleasure.

This, and the Advanced Award which followed in 1973, serves an admirable purpose and we strongly recommend that every beginner tries for the LTPA as his or her first achievement and the Advanced Award as his second.

The LTPA test, which has to be given by an official examiner, and for which a fee is charged, requires anyone taking it to score 28 out of a possible 42 points. The full test is as follows:

Section 1

Forehand drives
> 5 fed from service line—to be returned into Singles Court.
> 5 fed from base line—to be returned into Singles Court.

Backhand drives
> 5 fed from service line—to be returned into Singles Court.
> 5 fed from base line—to be returned into Singles Court.

Services
> 5 pairs from right court—first or second serve to count.
> 5 pairs from left court—first or second serve to count.

Forehand volleys
> 3 easy balls from base line—to be returned into Singles Court.

Backhand volleys
> 3 easy balls from base line—to be returned into Singles Court.

Alternate volleys
> 6 alternate forehand and backhand volleys of greater difficulty fed to simulate a 6 stroke rally—to be returned into the Singles Court.

Section 2

Rallies
> 4 rallies, Examiner varying length, pace and direction.
> Examiner's errors do not count.
> The Examiner starts each rally.

A rally of 10 strokes is required—maximum attempts 4. A PASS if one rally reaches 10 strokes, including those of the examiner.

Section 3

Two games with Examiner (each serves for 1 game) with the player calling the score.
Ability to score—YES/NO
YES is a PASS in Section 3.

Section 4

Assessment, based on the above two games, of player's ability to play a game.
POOR/FAIR/GOOD.
A PASS if the assessment is FAIR or GOOD.
The applicant will be given a receipt for the fee, and will be informed of the result by the Examiner immediately after the examination.
The Lawn Tennis Registered Professional Coaches' Association will send a Certificate and LTPA Badge to successful examinees.

In the Advanced Award, A PASS is obtained by a score in Section 1 of 35; a 20-stroke rally; and a Game Assessment of GOOD. An Advanced Certificate and a white, instead of yellow, badge are awarded to successful candidates. All other procedure is exactly the same as for the first Award.

Having achieved your proficiency badges, your next step should be to join a club. In doing so, always remember you should be giving to fellow members just as much as you are receiving.
It is generally simple to join a club. A local sports dealer will usually be able to name one or two in the vicinity and if he fails, a list can be obtained from the Lawn Tennis Association. Contact should then be made with the club

secretary. He will tell how to join the club; normally a proposer and seconder are needed, but most clubs will sum up an applicant during an interview and in many cases arrange for a proposer and seconder to be found.

When attending the club for the first time be friendly but not too pushful. Be happy to go on court with anybody and everybody, and inspire everyone with your enthusiasm. Enter the club tournaments and ask the club secretary or captain to provide partners for the doubles events. Do not be too proud to help the youngest member nor too intimidated to make up a four with the club champion. Obey the club rules and above all be friendly with everyone. This quickly leads to happy relationships and many pleasurable evenings and weekends will surely follow.

Competitive sport in all forms now plays such an important part in the life of this country that it is generally forgotten that rules were originally framed not to stop people from cheating but to help the enjoyment of perfectly fair-minded people playing games.

This is the spirit which should be observed when playing in a club and, indeed, when taking part in tournaments. This notion may be contrary to the popular idea that 'killer instinct' is an absolute essential in everybody and that 'win at all costs' is the only spirit in which to play matches.

These theories are in direct conflict with the characters of most of the Wimbledon winners since the very foundation of those championships. Apart from any ethical consideration, cheating, or its near companion 'gamesmanship', breeds a tiny character, in contrast to a more sporting attitude which inevitably breeds bigness of spirit and performance.

Serving before the opponent is ready, influencing the linesmen or umpire by glaring or shaking the head, talking to opponents during change of ends, these are typical manoeuvres of many present-day, would-be champions who have been trained in the theory that victory is the only thing which matters.

Even those who believe in this theory will surely comprehend that such an attitude in ordinary club play can only lead to friction and serious loss of enjoyment, both for themselves and for everyone with whom they play.

Another all too common and unfortunate sight is the man who shakes his head, growls, or generally looks disgusted and angry whenever his partner puts the ball into the net or hits it out of court. This kind of attitude is useless. Logic suggests that everyone on a tennis court is doing his or her best to play as well as possible and that mistakes are even more infuriating to their makers than to partners.

It is only common sense, therefore, to do everything possible to encourage partners to produce their best form and to feel absolutely relaxed and at ease. No matter how brilliantly one partner may play, victory against a comparable pair will only be achieved if the other half of the team is playing up to normal standard. The handful of spectators may applaud individual acts of brilliance but the record books show only the winning pair. Irrespective of any questions of victory or defeat, there is tremendous satisfaction to be obtained from encouraging and helping an off-colour partner to find his best form.

It is sometimes difficult to decide which partner shall serve first, especially if the sun is shining strongly at one end of the court. Who shall play in which court is another frequent cause of uncertainty. If such questions cannot easily be resolved, the quickest and fairest way to settle them is by spinning a racket or coin: 'Heads I play in the right court, Tails you play in it'.

Occasionally players set up partnerships only to find that, no matter how hard they try, their temperaments are incompatible. In such circumstances it is far better to discuss the problem openly and amicably and then sever the partnership than to go on growling inwardly while attempting to continue it. In fact, such honest discussions frequently disperse the incompatibilities which originally led to them.

Tennis is one of the few games in which men and women can take part together on more or less equal terms. This does not apply to singles because a man of good standard will always be superior to a woman whose standing in a national or club ranking is roughly comparable. In mixed doubles, however, the mixed sexes are complementary.

Nevertheless, the man should always show due consideration towards his partner when entering or leaving the court or when changing from one end to the other. Because he may be hitting the ball as hard as possible at the opposing woman in a few seconds time it does not mean he should rudely brush past her when passing from one end of the court to the other.

Whether or not it is permissible to hit the ball hard and straight at the opposing woman is a decision which must be taken individually by each player. Certainly the fact that a woman is on the same court as a man implies her willingness to play on level terms and so she is expecting some shots to be hit straight at her. Nevertheless, there can be little excuse for an absolute barrage of bodyline drives when many other possibilities are open.

Serving or hitting hard in the normal way or even continuous use of drop shots is perfectly permissible and no woman worthy of her salt would wish to be spared these examples of her opponents' skill. Skill is a different thing from brutality.

In tournaments it is clearly perfectly legitimate to wear out the opponent during play. However, it is unsporting not to return balls from the backstop directly to him when he is waiting for them to serve and you should make sure of retrieving a full share of balls from the net itself.

It is perfectly fair to lob directly into the sun during a rally but somewhat shady to return balls from one end of the court to the other between rallies by hitting them up into the sun. In a nutshell, everything legitimate is fair during a rally play and should be attempted. Between points you should treat opponents with the consideration you expect from them in return.

Behaviour in the clubhouse should correspond with the behaviour you would expect from visitors to your own home. Be natural and easy at all times.

It is the responsibility of every club member to obey the club rules, not only in the letter but in the spirit, and to encourage other members to do the same thing. Remember that committees have a pretty thankless job and that everything should be done to make their task easy. Take a full share of bar duty or in sweeping or otherwise preparing the courts. Be ready to travel to other clubs in order to support the club team in match play. Many worthwhile friendships have been started in this way.

To sum it all up, do everything possible to foster friendliness and club spirit. The foregoing applies to all age groups but people in their teens are soon likely to look beyond their club tournaments and inter-club matches for competition. Tournaments, senior and junior, which have no restrictions on entries are the obvious stepping stones.

Some of the bigger ones do not prevent anyone from sending in an entry form. However, there is often a selection committee which decides from details on the entry form and general knowledge about form, who is and who is not sufficiently good to merit acceptance. Quite a few present-day tournaments leave some blank spaces which they fill from survivors among the 'not-quite-good-enoughs' who are given the chance to compete in a preliminary, qualifying event staged just before the tournament proper begins.

Each year in England the Lawn Tennis Association sanctions about 60 Senior and 160 Junior tournaments.

Full lists and dates, with the names and addresses of secretaries, are available annually. Simply send your request, with a stamped and addressed envelope, to: The Secretary, Lawn Tennis Association, Barons Court, London W14 9EG. The Scottish LTA and the associations of each of the 100 or so member nations of the International Lawn Tennis Federation issue similar lists. The names and addresses of their secretaries are published each year in the LTA Official Handbook, a copy of which is sent to the secretary of every affiliated club.

Once you have decided which tournaments are convenient or suitable for you, write to the appropriate secretaries for entry forms.

Many people are shy about entering tournaments, but we strongly advise you not to be so. There will be many others like you and quite soon—say after a couple of tournaments—you will begin to feel in the swim.

In any case, most junior tournaments nowadays promote events with upper age limits of 21, 18 and 16, and the 14- and 12-year-old groups grow in size season by season. We are wondering who will be first with an 8 and Under event.

At one time the age limit meant the competitor had to be under the age on the day the tournament began. Now the general habit all round the world is to set the age limit against the first day of the year just beginning. Thus children born on or after 1 January 1974 are eligible for 18 and Under events up to and including the year 1992. However, the entry form will normally stipulate the requirements.

Over the past ten years there has been an increase in tournaments that do not appear on lists issued by the LTA. The Nestlé National School Tournament, the BP Shield Championship, the London Parks & Clubs Association, the GLC, the London *Evening News,* the National Association of Women's Institutes, many provincial and local newspapers, and nearly every County LTA stage competitions, to say nothing of tennis schools. To discover just what is happening in your area, contact your liveliest sports dealer or your County LTA Honorary Secretary or the registered coaches in your district.

Lawn Tennis magazine has sponsored a few experimental tournaments in schools and similar establishments. These have sought to analyse the effectiveness of different scoring, of special training systems, and so on, and have resulted in the introduction of the round-robin system in a number of junior tournaments. This means that competitors are put together in groups in which each person plays all others in his group.

In a normal draw half the players are eliminated after one match and a further quarter after another match. If there are thirty-two players originally, sixteen play once, eight twice, four three times, and two play four times.

Now divide the thirty-two into eight groups of four in which all play all. Every competitor is assured of three matches, the group winners a further one, two, three or four, depending on how the event is then completed. The group is won by the player with most victories.

So this system is preferable for moderate players who are travelling far to compete in a tournament for they know they will meet at least three different opponents.

Another system makes every single point played by each competitor affect who ultimately wins the tournament. It is called 'medal play' and is based on golf where every shot counts. As in the round-robin system, players are put into groups in which all play all. But instead of using traditional scoring, the first player to win 31 points wins the match.

His result is entered not as W (for won) or L (for lost) followed by the score but simply by a number. If he is the winner, the number is 31, *plus* the difference between his score and the loser's, *plus* 5 for winning. The loser is simply given the points he scored.

Suppose William beat James 31–23. William would have beside his name 31 + 8 (31 − 23) + 5, which is 44. James would score 23.

The beauty of this system is that a player who just wins all his matches can still finish behind another who may lose once or even twice but wins his other matches very easily.

Furthermore, the player who won all his matches may well lose first place because of two or three careless mistakes against the weakest player in the group. So 100 per cent concentration from start to finish and from all players is vital. It is a severely testing system for groups training for tournament play.

8 Equipment and clothing

There are three reasons for taking care about the clothes you wear for playing tennis. They are:

1 so that you can move easily
2 so you look the part; this helps confidence considerably
3 so that you are either protected against the cold, or perspiration can be suitably absorbed in heat.

Ease of movement starts in a knowledgeable choice of the clothes you will be wearing, both for practice and match play; remember tournament successes are gained on the practice court. Most players use up their old clothes when practising, but if these have become too tight or stiff they can easily bring about restrictions which alter the grooving of your strokes or movements without your realizing it.

Worn shoes, too-short laces, shrunken shirts, loose-waisted shorts or skirts, voluminous skirts or sweaters, too-tight socks with holes, over-tight shorts or pants; all these are liable to detract from your best performance in practice. Do not be penny wise and pound foolish. Throw them out.

Shoes

Starting at the feet then, what kind of a mover are you? Are you nimble and light of foot or ponderous and slow? Are you comfortable when sliding or do you feel more confident when your foothold is completely secure? Do your feet bruise easily or can you run barefoot on pebbles?

Think about all these things before going to a well-stocked shop to make your purchase. Be sure it has adequate equipment for discovering your correct size and fitting. If you can afford it, we recommend that you buy two pairs of shoes at a time, once having established that the first pair are completely comfortable. They should be identical, so that you can alternate them match by match. Buying cheap, poorly made gym shoes is one of the poorest investments you can make. Once your game starts to form, you will run many miles per week on the court, giving your feet a tremendous pounding. They need all the protection and support you can give them. It is not feasible to give exact prices in this book, but you are unlikely to find a pair of high-grade tennis shoes much under £3; if you are very extravagant you can spend as much as £10 on an imported pair. They look better and will last longer if you clean them immediately after wear.

We do not know of any juniors who willingly go on court with shoes that are too small, but many play regularly in shrunken socks thinking that they will stretch. Maybe they will but not before they have damaged your feet. Maybe the damage is so slight that it will pass unnoticed after any one match, but repetition can easily cause permanent discomfort or injury. This takes no account of things like corns, bunions and athlete's foot, all of which seem to thrive on small or dirty socks.

So when buying socks, first be absolutely sure that they are big enough and pre-shrunk. All wool socks tend to shrink quicker than those knitted with man-made fibres, but these are non-absorbent. Therefore, we recommend socks made from a combination of both. The chain stores usually have a good variety.

For girls who are still growing, we recommend a skirt and shirt combination. Many of the leading manufacturers offer neat all-round pleated skirts with a Velcro expandable waistline at sensible prices. These look smart and practical when worn with any of the better cotton sports shirts readily available. Here we would advise you to buy from either a registered professional or a reputable sports dealer because either will take care to sell you shirts that are long enough not to ride up and have non-restricting armholes.

Boys can wear similar shirts. The cut of shorts varies slightly from make to make. When all other things are equal, select a pair with side adjustments to allow for growing.

Sweaters

All clothing other than your sweaters should be the regulation white (or cream) even though they may have coloured trimmings. However, as from 1 January 1974, the Lawn Tennis Association allowed tournament committees freedom to permit light colours to be introduced. Sweaters of varying colours have been fashionable for almost a hundred years, so here you can allow your imagination greater freedom.

Ensure that the sweater you buy is loose, not floppy, and that it gives maximum protection against the wind. Make it your absolute rule to put on your sweater immediately after finishing every match or practice session. Failing to do so is the quickest possible way of developing stiffness and chills, with sprains and muscle tearings as the first sequel.

Underclothes and accessories

What you wear underneath is just as important as top clothing, beginning with over-knickers. These should be neither too tight nor too loose fitting. They are always seen during play, whether your choice is tailored or lace-trimmed and should be worn over your briefs.

All underclothes worn next to your skin, whether you be a boy or a girl, should ideally be of absorbent cotton.

If you insist on having long hair which flops over your eyes, be sure to wear either a towelling headband, hair grips, or ribbons. You may think long hair looks attractive, but it is uncomfortable for strenuous play.

It was once generally believed that you should use as heavy a racket as possible. This has been proved now to be incorrect, so our first piece of advice when choosing a racket is to put ease of handling as your top priority.

Using a JUNIOR racket (this is usually printed on the frame) will not soften your shots because the ease with which you will be able to swing it will outweigh the lack of an ounce or two of weight. The grip should be square-shaped as in figure 21a, rather than oblong as in figure 21b, and should be as large as you can comfortably manage. This reduces arm strain and so helps to protect you from excessive tiredness and tennis elbow.

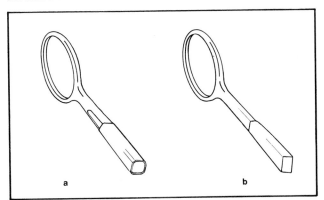

21 Tennis-racket grips

There are two types of junior racket: one with a shorter handle than the regular racket, and the other 2 inches shorter still. So that you may be quite sure which is which, the Slazenger Panther Club model (for up to eight years) measures 24½ inches from tip of racket head to end of handle, and the Dunlop Maxply Junior (for nine-eleven) is 26 inches in overall length. A Slazenger Challenger Power racket measures 27 inches.

Racket strings are made either from sheep or lamb's gut or man-made fibres. The former have greater elasticity, which allows longer contact between ball and racket when making strokes. This increases the 'feel' you experience and so helps control and power. Man-made fibres lack elasticity but are much harder wearing. Beginners are usually happy with nylon stringing but advanced players prefer the more responsive animal gut. Lamb's gut is best because it transmits sensations of touch to the brain with greater surety.

To compensate for the reduced elasticity of man-made strings, have your racket strung 10 per cent less tightly than when using animal gut. If you find 50 lb of tension with lamb's gut right but you need to use nylon for economic reasons, have your racket strung to 45 lb tension.

A racket is your tool of the trade so show yourself to be a true craftsman in the way you treat it. Always keep it in a cover when travelling to and from playing. When it is not actually in use, keep it in a cool, dry place—*and in a press*. There are few things more depressing in tennis than spending £10 on a racket, failing to care for it, and then suddenly discovering just before a match that it has warped out of shape. Wipe the strings with a dry cloth after use in a damp atmosphere. Take care of the grip. Avoid hitting the ground, especially in anger.

As with rackets, so with clothes. Wash them the moment they look the slightest bit grubby; that is one reason for buying drip-dry material. Keep them, neatly folded, in a clean dry spot when not in use.

Inspect your shoe strings each time you clean them; it is seriously disturbing when one snaps at a critical point of a match and you are without a replacement. But all this is concerned with behaviour, another all-important factor.

Psychologists have long known that if you feel angry and excited inside, this will affect how your face looks. Recently they have discovered that if you are calm but look irritable, your look will quickly upset your calm interior. Anger, irritability, nervousness, etc., all mar good performance. So, for your own sake, look calm and stay calm. If you feel your hackles rising, count slowly to ten, take two or three *slow, deep* breaths and make yourself look tranquil. Apart from the beneficial effect this will have on you, it will deprive your opponent of any lift he might receive from seeing you are ruffled or cross.

Practice this assiduously and soon people will begin praising you for your calmness. This will strengthen your inner resolve, you will increase your inner serenity, more people will talk of your calmness, you will be more resolute as a result—and the cycle progresses.

On no account should you fall into the habit of 'hamming it up', swearing, arguing with the umpire, and so on in order to be in the swim. If other people behave stupidly that is their right or, better, misfortune.

You are *you*. You are an individual human being and you should always behave like one. When you slip, which is probable, recover your composure as quickly as possible, push the incident into the back of your mind, and vow to yourself it will never happen again.

If you have to play a match and are nervous, be thankful—you are keyed up and ready for action. Make the nervousness work for you. Do this by concentrating on what you are trying to do. Probably you will feel flutterings in your tummy. Perhaps you will suffer slight breathlessness and leaden legs. Your arm may stiffen. If so, sacrifice a couple of games by hitting every shot as hard as you can—a few shots may go in and demoralize your opponent. Fix your mind on something definite like hitting each ball just after it has gone over the top of the bounce.

Above all, enjoy the challenge and the game itself. Even if, one day, you find yourself playing for a £10,000 prize, still remember tennis is a game to enjoy and that enjoyment makes you play better rather than worse.

9 Coaching and more advanced play

We are convinced that it is advantageous to receive coaching right from the start and, if you are young, in a group rather than as an individual.

So far this book has been much concerned with beginners, the ways in which they can become proficient, and the best methods open to parents or other helpers to help them develop on sound lines which will lead on to further improvement.

Thanks to the generous sponsorship of the Green Shield Trading Stamp Company, subsidized, low-price coaching has become available all over the country. In the mid-1970s some 25,000 children a year were attending the many centres. These centres begin with the basic ball sense tests covered in our early chapters and go on to the fundamental strokes of the game. The courses are usually of six lessons and in many counties there are follow-up chances of further tuition and play.

However, we are strongly of the opinion that each individual must help himself. So we advise readers to plan their own follow-ups. In terms of coaching, this normally means going to a man or woman who possesses some recognized qualifications, either as a coach or player.

So far as coaches are concerned, especially at all levels leading up to junior champion standard, you are scarcely likely to better a member of the Lawn Tennis Registered Professional Coaches' Association. All members have either acquired great experience through many years of teaching or, in the case of newer members, through a testing apprenticeship, three courses and three stiff examinations.

Again, we favour group rather than individual lessons for young players—for older ones, too, until they become reasonably proficient and have reached the level of the Lawn Tennis Advanced Proficiency Badge. Learning in groups removes the loneliness, and so the immense consciousness of your own failures, of individual lessons. In a group you are likely to find fellow pupils as error-prone as yourself and in no time at all each member of the group is usually laughing at all mistakes, including his own—and also enjoying everyone's good shots.

Contrary to popular opinion this is the main Australian system, the aim being to give everyone great pleasure and love of the game. The coaches watch very carefully and pupils with special talents are noted. If they progress as expected, the coach will wait until they are about fourteen years old and then approach the parents concerning the chances of their becoming a good or even top-class competitor; that is when individual coaching tends to start.

The leap from proficiency badge holder to county junior champion is big, but well within the teaching capabilities of most, perhaps all, members of the LTRPCA. It is when the champion standard is achieved that a major problem is liable to arise. This is the moment when the county, regional, or national junior talent spotting officials are likely to make approaches with subsidized or completely free coaching, special courses, and so on.

Let us issue a warning. It concerns a trap which, in our combined seventy years of experience, we have seen nine out of every ten sets of parents fall into, so we want to stress it:

Being offered free coaching or any other form of official help never means you have arrived. The squad is not the

*end but only one tiny step towards it. So treat such invitations
with reserve and keep them in true perspective. Little
Johnny, who was not invited, may still end up the swan and
your offspring the goose.*

Even when there is full understanding, there are still
pitfalls, the most important of which concerns the danger
of changing coaches. All too often a qualified coach
discovers a promising beginner whom he guides and
helps to become county junior champion. Along come the
official 'sifters' who pick him for, say, national training.

The parents may be aware of the danger set out above
but they are pleased, flattered even, by the invitation.
Understandably, they consider that national training
must be superior to the work of tennis 'GPs' working in
the provinces or suburbs.

Alas, this just isn't the case—and this casts no reflection
upon national or regional coaches. There is no question of
ability at stake here, only of relationships. Effective
coaching depends more on power of communication and
rapport than on any other factors, always assuming an
adequacy of basic technical efficiency in the coach. The
pupil must possess faith in his teacher and faith—deep,
lasting faith—takes time to grow. By and large, a coach
who helps a pupil rise from beginner to junior champion
will have gained that faith. Maybe he is not a coaching
genius. Perhaps the man who would be in charge of the
national or regional squad possesses superior knowledge
and skill, viewed dispassionately. But only if he is a genius
will he fail to create conflicts in the pupil who, anyway,
will be suffering inner doubts at leaving the coach who has
taken him so far.

Also, the likelihood of the official coach devoting as
much time and thought to the new pupil as the personal
coach is remote. So in an overwhelming majority of
cases, 'promotion' to a national coaching-training level
has meant only one thing—failure. This was dramatically
emphasized in 1973 when two members of the 100 per

cent subsidized national squad paid substantial fees to receive coaching from our school advanced coaches. Their improved results and consequent earnings more than covered their expenditure.

Therefore, unless there are irrefutable reasons for change, our advice is to stay with your own coach rather than to go to a regional or national scheme.

Be gracious and grateful for any offers. Ask if it is possible to make use of the facilities and practice but explain that you wish for your own coach to continue training you. Better be confident and progress slowly with him than to switch and go backwards. Thankfully, there is growing acceptance of this approach and we are hopeful that in the near future increased efforts will be made to coach the coaches instead of promising players.

Returning to coaching and the Green Shield scheme, the National Sports Council, the Boys' Schools LTA, the Girls' Schools LTA, some parks authorities, many coaches, Saturday mornings at clubs and so on, offer between them facilities for a wide range of courses.

British Petroleum are sponsoring an important incentive scheme in which winners of junior age group single events at tournaments qualify for junior membership of the BP International Fellowship. You can recognize these youngsters by the green badge and racket-head covers inscribed with the letters BPITF. Once you have gained such a badge you become eligible for their winter physical fitness programme and their group coaching sessions, which are usually conducted by one of nine world-famous stars of the calibre of Ken Rosewall, Roger Taylor or Mark Cox. Additionally, BP stage a large tournament which spreads itself over the summer for badge holders and they are promoting an ever-increasing number of matches between the best British junior members of the Fellowship and the top juniors from other countries. As an example—the series staged on the covered courts at the Palace Hotel, Torquay, in February 1974 covered eight countries for the boys and four for the girls. So these competitions provide a big incentive for any youngster to prepare for, and win, a group event.

So just to remind any ambitious reader: first find out where convenient tournaments are held. Enter them and then do your very best to win an event. When you have achieved this, write as soon as possible and tell John Barrett, P.O. Box 10, Wimbledon SW19. You will then have two feet on the first rung of the ladder of success.

Should you have difficulty in contacting tournament organizers or learning where the events are staged, send to your county LTA or see your liveliest local sports goods dealer for fuller details. If still in doubt, write to the Lawn Tennis Association at Barons Court, London W14 9EG.

It is possible for you to reach this standard through group lessons and carefully thought-out practice, but now perhaps comes the time for you to seek the more refined coaching only obtainable through individual tuition. Winning a tournament means you are crossing the bridge linking all the fun and *camaraderie* of group lessons with the more challenging, though no less pleasurable, demands of strict competitive tennis. This is the stage where your brain and character are going to be exercised as much as, or even more than, your arms, legs and eyes.

In group lessons you learned in general terms how to hit the ball. In an individual lesson the coach will be able to give you in ever-increasing amounts the refinements of technique which separate juniors from good seniors, good seniors from senior tournament competitors and senior tournament competitors from winners of tournaments, national championships and international open events, like Bournemouth, Forest Hills, Melbourne, Madrid, Rome, Hamburg, Paris and Wimbledon.

Not only will he teach you how to execute an increasing repertoire of strokes, but he will tell you when and why. Simultaneously he can teach you tactics, varying from the comparatively simple changes of pace and angle which are effective in junior tennis to the complicated psychological warfare carried out on the Wimbledon Centre Court during the All-England Championships.

Since you will already have won your first age-group event, the coach will probably begin at an intermediate level. What does this mean? He will begin by assessing you as an individual and decide what is best for you. As there are approximately one million players in Britain, each one different, we cannot possibly tell you what he will say to you. Instead, we will give as an example the coaching plan made for Ashley White, one of Britain's better juniors, in the mid-1970s.

These are the relevant passages from our briefing of the coach of our selection, Jasmat Dhiraj, at the start of 1974:

He must develop:

1 the ability to keep the ball in play
2 the determination to chase every ball
3 the ability to hit the strokes he has learned as confidently on the run as he does from a static position.

Intermediate coaching leads imperceptibly into advanced coaching. Like the intermediate stage, this will be tailored to suit your personal needs by any skilled coach. Again, it is impossible to generalize but we are absolutely certain of the immense value of sequence tennis.

This is founded on the fact that many situations in tennis constantly recur, so these are used as the start of one or the other of a series of set routines. Your coach can help you develop these by feeding the ball to the spots indicated in the diagrams, starting off with 'A' on your side of the court. These points have been designed with varying objects in mind, such as exploiting weaknesses, breaking down strength, creating uncertainty, sapping stamina and perhaps most important of all, increasing your own confidence to a point where it is almost inviolate against the ravages of stress, nervousness and tiredness.

Sig. 6

Before detailing some of these sequences, let us warn you that some critics will tell you that such sequences will make you an unthinking player. Our answer is that even Einstein began with his twice times table and has the world ever produced a more brilliantly creative scientist and mathematician? Similarly, once you have a ground-work of completely reliable sequences which you have practised so diligently that they have become almost automatic, your mind will be free to work imaginatively and spontaneously. Now for the sequences.

In each of these, you play your first shot from 'A'. Your opponent may only return the ball to the spot around 'C' about 50 per cent of the time. If it is not possible for you then to make the shot you planned, simply remain patient and start all over again at the next opportunity.

Forehand side

Many returns from your opponent will come fairly deep towards your forehand. Each one gives you the opportunity to start a choice of sequences. These are a few:

22 ·Short forehand
cross-court shot, followed
by a deep forehand
down the line.
Follow it up to the net.
Note distance opponent
has to run backwards
(shown by double line)

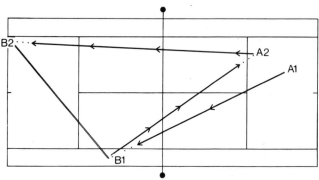

———————————▶
Flight of ball

══════════════
Run backwards

· · ·
Ball after bounce

You will meet many opponents who continually run up to the net. Sometimes it is very difficult to pass them or to keep them on the baseline. So accept that they will be advancing to the net but make it as difficult as possible for them to gain an advantage by using a sequence of two wide-angled shots to start with.

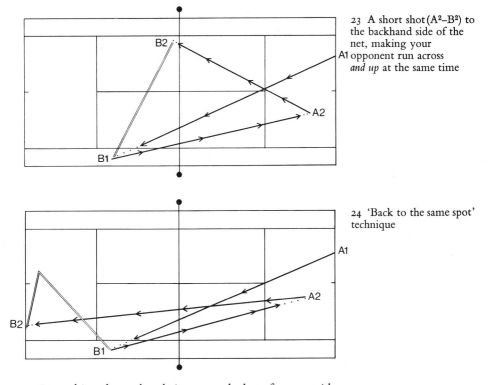

23 A short shot (A²–B²) to the backhand side of the net, making your opponent run across *and up* at the same time

24 'Back to the same spot' technique

By making them play their approach shots from outside the tramlines you force them to rush across the net to cover the gaping hole at their side of the net. This leaves you with the choice of hitting your passing shot towards the gap or of lobbing it in the air over the gap; or finally deep back to the same side from which they are rushing. If you mix these cleverly, it won't take you long to have the net-rusher completely bewildered and baffled.

Backhand side
The majority of returns are aimed to your backhand wing, the ball bouncing somewhere between the base and service lines. These also provide opportunities for a number of sequences:

25 A short angled drive to
the forehand followed by
a short angled drive to
the backhand, making
your opponent run the full
width of the court

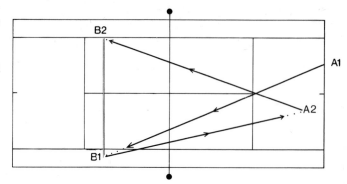

26 Backhand cross-court
shot followed by a
backhand down the line.
Follow it up to the net for
the volley finish.

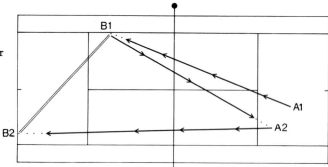

27 Backhand cross-court
shot followed by a
backhand short shot
down the line.
Follow it up to the net
(instead of retreating) for a
volley finish.

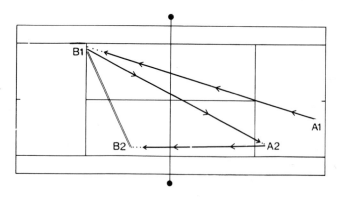

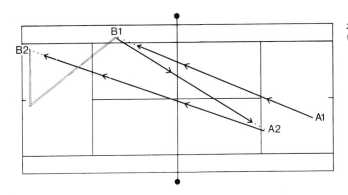

28 'Back to the same spot' technique

To repel the net-rusher with your backhand, use sequence in figure 29:

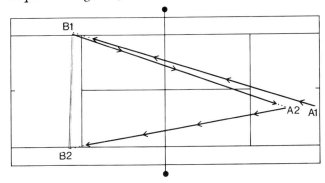

29 Short angled shot to the backhand followed by a short shot angled to the forehand. If your opponent rushes the net on either of his shots you have a choice of replies similar to those given in 25.

10 Tactics

By now you should have a good idea of how all the basic strokes are produced. If you have followed all our instructions and a parent or friend has been keeping a watchful and helpful eye, you may have become quite proficient in their production. So, having learned how to make the shots, your next task is to learn when and where to hit them. This is known as tactics.

There are eight golden rules for match play:

1 So far as you can, eliminate all unnecessary errors. Double faults are a special sin.

2 Chase everything, even if you think it's hopeless. You will undoubtedly surprise yourself with the number of 'impossibilities' you start returning when you try really hard.

3 To enable you to chase 'impossibilities' successfully, run with your racket out ready to hit the ball. Do not wait until you reach the ball before starting your swing.

4 Do not waste nine out of ten first services by trying to hit too hard. Slow down a little so that three-quarters of them are good ones. Most of your opponents will automatically think a first service is better than a second, so they will be more defensive than when your first service is a fault and you lollipop over a weak second service.

5 Even the softest return *over* the net is better than a more stylish drive *into* the net. So never miss returning service into court. Better still, aim to place the ball

within one yard of the baseline. When you can hit to this depth at will you will be extremely difficult to beat.

6 Learn to vary your length, as most players become better if you feed them with the same type of shot all the time. Always remember that no match is ever won until it is lost and vice-versa.

7 If you do your best with every ball that comes across the net to you, victories will surely follow.

8 Never give your opponent a shot he likes, if you can possibly avoid it.

These rules are so important that some of them need amplifying:

Unnecessary mistakes If you study any good analysis of an important match you will learn that even Wimbledon champions make more mistakes than winning shots, so it is very important that you do not present your opponents with strings of mistakes of shots you should never miss. Such mistakes usually arise because you subconsciously think 'this is easy' and relax your concentration slightly before hitting the ball. Never reduce your effort until you have actually won the point.

Some mistakes are inevitable because of the pressure your opponent may apply. Such mistakes are increased when you lack the knowledge of how to deal with such pressure.

This is where our 'zoning system' can help you immensely.

Wasteful serving When is it that your opponent is powerless to put pressure on you?—it can only be when you are serving. This is also a shot which you can practise without an opponent. There is simply no excuse for failing to practise your service, but do not concentrate simply on first services. As a player is only as good as his second service, make sure yours is better than most. A special tip about second services: the nearer they fall to the service

30 The 'Zoning System'

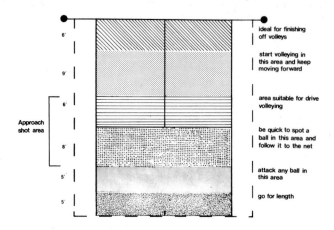

line the better. Turn back to Chapter 4 for a reminder of the many ways in which you can practise serving.

Varying length Most players, young and old, are more certain of their shots when running to and fro across the court than when they are forced to move forwards and backwards. This is why you should be able to tease mistakes out of your opponents by skilfully mixing long and short shots.

If you have sufficient ball control, keep the short returns low to make it more difficult for your opponent to hit an aggressive return. When making him run backwards, hit the ball high over the net so that he has to return it from well behind the baseline, possibly when he is still off balance. Once you become expert in changing your length you will find extra benefit in also varying the speed of your shots. However, make your changes of length and your variations of pace subtle. If you hit a fast drive and then a very slow one, the difference will be very clear; a medium-paced shot followed by one either a shade slower or faster is not so apparent and is more likely to upset your opponent's timing.

Be careful. Maybe he is also reading this book and will be trying the same tactics as you. If he is using a mixture of long and short shots, remember when running forward, his baseline is coming nearer so reduce the length of your shot accordingly. It is a common failure to over-hit the baseline on these changes of length.

Concentration Treat each ball on its merits. We frequently hear players talking about how they will win a match or a set. Sometimes you hear them say 'I must win this point'. It is our experience that every single shot you play needs all your concentration, so think only of the ball that is coming towards you and how best you can reply to it.

Some will be deep and fast and it will need every scrap of your skill and willpower merely to return them into court, while hoping the next shot will be easier. Others will seem so simple that you begin thinking the point has already been won and you make a silly mistake. So make it your rule that as soon as possible after your opponent has hit the ball, you decide what kind of a shot it is and how you are going to treat it. Then concentrate your mind completely on carrying out your decision. All this sounds elaborate but once your shots are reasonably automatic, you will be able to do it in a fraction of a second.

Knowing your opponent Never giving your opponent a shot he likes means you must have a sound knowledge of his game. If you are a keen and thorough competitor you will have analysed him before you go on court and written down in detail his strengths and weaknesses in a notebook. You will have then consulted this record before going on court.

However, there will be occasions when this is not possible. In this situation take special care to warm up before going on court so that you can use the knock-up to test out his game instead of grooving your own; that is why you should go on a practice court in advance.

Start the knock-up by hitting a medium-paced ball straight to him. The chances are strong that he will move to return it with his favourite shot. So if he hits a forehand it is likely he is not so happy when making backhands.

To see if this is correct, hit the next two or three balls to his backhand, taking a careful look to see how he shapes at them. Next try hitting a few soft, high returns to his baseline to learn how he deals with such 'nothing balls'.

Then hit a few very short shots to see if he moves readily to the net after hitting them. This should tell you how willingly or otherwise he volleys. When he is at the net, mix fast and slow shots to see which he handles most confidently and remember to hit two or three straight at him. Toss a few lobs over his head, both to the forehand and the backhand, to test the power and accuracy of his smashing.

He will probably be happy when hurrying from side to side to hit forehand, backhand, forehand, backhand, and so on. But what happens when you start him running and then send two balls in succession to the same spot as in diagrams 24 and 28 in Chapter 9? Few players are completely happy when hitting the ball after being made to turn; the change of direction and pace often upsets their balance and rhythm unless they are particularly lightfooted and agile. This is known as wrong-footing your opponent.

Drop shots and lobs. There is no softer shot in tennis than the one which drops the ball just over the net—the drop shot. Because this is soft, do not imagine it is defensive. Properly executed, it is one of the most aggressive shots in the game because it brings the opponent helter-skelter to the net, leaving him wide open to a ball lobbed in the air above reach of his racket before falling near the baseline. This sends him racing back and leaves him wide open to another drop shot, followed by yet another lob. That great master of tactics, Jaroslav Drobny—he won Wimbledon in 1954—was particularly skilled in using these tactics and in his heyday sent many an opponent off court exhausted.

Although the drop shot is delicate, it should be played when the oncoming ball is still rising after bouncing, or, at the latest, at the top of the bounce. Waiting longer than this usually advertises your intention and lengthens the time your opponent has to run in, besides giving him the chance to start moving earlier than if you hit the ball on the rise.

To make the ball die quicker once it has landed, give it a little underspin by sliding your racket under the ball in the manner described for low volleys in Chapter 5. We advise making drop shots straight ahead of you instead of across the court, to reduce the time the ball is in the air to a minimum. This gives your opponent less time to see what is happening.

There are two kinds of lobs—aggressive and defensive. Again, most people think of a lob as defensive but, skilfully executed at the correct moment, it is as aggressive as the fastest net-skimming drive to a corner. However, in matchplay, three lobs out of every four are normally made on the defensive. Such lobs should be hit as high and long as possible. This gives you time to return to a central position on court, while the height makes the ball fall straight downwards. It is much more difficult to time a ball falling perpendicularly out of the air than one which is falling at an angle.

Aggressive lobs should be pitched off a rising ball in an arc which reaches its highest point immediately above the net. See figure 31.

Intangibles Once you become a regular tournament competitor, you will discover that strokes and tactics

31 Aggressive lobs (path a) should be hit flat or with slight top spin so that the apex of the arc is over the net. Then a ball hit from baseline b1 must, on a calm day, come down on baseline b2. Defensive lobs d should be hit higher and with back spin. This changes the path of the ball to d. The last part of the descent is almost perpendicular and this increases the opponent's timing problem. Such lobs must be high—30 feet or more—and hit with enough strength to overcome the retarding effects of back spin so that the ball comes down near the baseline.

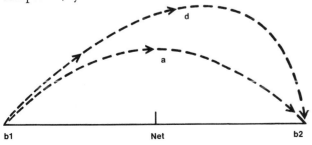

b1   Net   b2

are only half the story. In order to win matches, you will need courage, endurance, patience and, above all, a willingness to go on and on and on—no matter how badly you are losing. This is known as 'staying with the opponent'.

It is based on the knowledge that everybody has a breaking point. From the moment you start competitive play, make up your mind that it will always take your opponent longer to drive you beyond your breaking point than it will take you to crack his. One aspect of this can be summed up as 'I'll get it back or bust'. Every time you return a ball to him you are taking him one stroke nearer his breaking point while, in returning the ball, you are delaying your own breaking point by one stroke.

When you begin tournaments this can seem disheartening, possibly you will be playing someone who is three or four years older than you, much bigger and stronger physically and considerably more experienced in the game. It may seem that your efforts to scramble the ball back are a waste of time because he simply places each following shot in another difficult position and you still lose the points. No matter! Keep on trying!

Maybe he will still beat you easily but every now and again he won't! Perhaps he will become overconfident when he sees that you may be smaller than he is and so start experimenting with fancy shots. Perhaps he will miss one or two, or you will return them and eventually win a couple of games. This may annoy him and make him try to beat you quickly; too quickly, so that he starts making mistakes.

In the meantime, by trying hard, you will probably have improved your own game a little so that the gap between you has now narrowed. Given a little luck like a net-cord shot or a winning shot off the wood, it is possible that he will crack. This could end each season with your record showing a couple of wins over people who should have beaten you easily. Even if it doesn't, it is never too early to start trying your best for every shot.

11 How to win friends and matches

We should always treat others as we would wish to be treated ourselves. That is the essence of the etiquette which, when faithfully observed, makes tennis probably the most sporting and pleasurable game of all. In our experience, players come in two categories: 'Yes' or 'No' people. If you are a 'Yes' person, other people enjoy playing with or against you, even in intensely competitive matches. If you are a 'No' person, they do not enjoy playing with you and you are in for a lonely time at any club you join or tournament you enter.

Practically everyone we have come across wants to be a 'Yes' person and as we feel sure that you will too, here are twenty-four points of tennis etiquette which we hope will help you:

1 Before beginning play, always introduce yourself to the person in charge of the courts and ask to be assigned to one before walking on, even if there are several vacant and there is no charge for playing.

2 If you see a lowered net, remember its message may be 'please do not play on this court'. So never raise the net and begin playing without first obtaining permission.

3 If you have to cross behind or over courts on which other people are playing to reach the one to which you have been assigned, wait until the point is over, or maybe the game, before trying to reach your court.

Never cross behind the players or walk up the side while the ball is in play and, please, though you may be in a hurry, be sure always to shut the gate on entering or leaving the courts.

4 Introduce yourself in a clear voice to your opponent and, if it is a doubles, your partner, the moment you meet. Toss the racket for choice of end or service before beginning the warm up so you may move immediately to the end of the court on which you will begin play.

5 All players should practise their serves at the same time during the warm up, and not just before the set starts. This is not always the case in America, where it is acceptable for each player to hit his practice serves immediately before it is his turn to serve.

6 The rules of tennis were drawn up in order to help people obtain more pleasure out of the game. They were not intended to impose petty restrictions. It is unsporting and an insult to your opponent not to observe the rules strictly. When you inadvertently transgress, be the first to put it right. It is not unsporting to expect your opponent to be equally strict with himself in observing the spirit as well as the letter of the rules.

7 When you are not absolutely sure whether a ball is in or out, always play a let (that means replay the point). However, remember if even the tiniest fraction of the ball touches the line, it is a good shot.

8 If a ball rolling across the court distracts your opponent or he suffers any other kind of interference, always offer to play a let. Similarly, if it happens to you, do not attempt to continue the rally. Instead, ask the umpire, or your opponent, to play a let.

9 Once the rally has started, by all means hurry your opponent as much as you can, but never serve before he is ready. Always wait until everyone is in position before you serve. If your opponent serves before you

are ready ('quick serves') do not attempt to make a return, but call out 'I wasn't ready; please serve again'. However, it is your duty to take up a receiving position quickly and not to keep your opponents and partner waiting. If you are guilty of this you may be accused of stalling or gamesmanship, polite words for cheating.

10 Never be a chatterbox on court. Excessive talking is one of the most irritating breaches of etiquette.

11 You may be the best player but that doesn't excuse you from sharing the expense of buying balls.

12 All the balls should be within reach of the server so that the rule 'play must be continuous' can be observed.

13 Do not throw or hit a ball to anyone unless he is looking at you. Throw it so he does not have to bend or move unduly. It is bad form to roll a ball back to the players on the court next door while they are playing a point. Similarly, never interrupt a rally on another court to retrieve a loose ball. Always wait for the point to end and then collect the ball.

14 Try to pick up balls at the same time as your opponent because this saves valuable playing time.

15 Returning a first service unnecessarily when it is an obvious fault is a form of rudeness and it may, in certain situations, be considered gamesmanship.

16 When other people are waiting to play, either offer them your court at the end of a set or invite them to join in with you. Keep a watchful eye open for new-comers sitting around at the club or park at which you play, that they are not ignored and starved of games.

17 When the set or match finishes, don't just walk off the court. Be sure to thank your opponents and partner for the game and go around the netting to collect your share of the balls you have been using. If no one is waiting to come on the court, lower the net with three or four turns of the handle; this helps to lengthen its life.

18 When competing in a tournament, do your share of

calling lines or umpiring. There was once a good unwritten rule which required every competitor to umpire at least one match a day. If in doubt about what umpiring or line calling entails, make it your duty to visit the nearest big tournament to study this aspect of the game. If this is impractical, much information can be gathered by watching television during the Wimbledon fortnight.

19 Either when playing a match without an umpire or when umpiring or line judging for others, make any call of 'out' or 'let' instantaneously. Otherwise the ball will be presumed good and still in play.

20 Enjoy your match and occasionally say 'Good shot' to your opponent.

21 The committee and officials who run clubs and tournaments are almost always voluntary workers giving back to the game some of the goodness they derived from it themselves when younger. So be sure to thank them before you leave and to assist them in any way you can.

22 Never shout, swear, sulk or otherwise misbehave on court. Apart from being ill-mannered, such behaviour tells your opponent you are worried and encourages him.

23 Always be on time for your matches. It is only good manners to be so and, if it is a tournament, being late may result in the referee's defaulting you.

24 Over the entrance to Wimbledon's famous Centre Court are engraved Kipling's immortal words:

> If you can meet with Triumph and Disaster
> And treat those two Imposters just the same.

Whether you are a novice starting out on his very first tournament match or the World No. 1 contesting the final at Wimbledon, obeying the spirit of these words will not diminish your performance. It will also increase your enjoyment and that, after all, is what tennis is all about.